MW00934312

ACTIVITY MEMORY BOOK FOR ADULTS

With

Dementia, Alzheimer's, Senility, Cognitive Impairment, Parkinson's, Aphasia and other Neurodegenerative Diseases.

HARRISON MAXFIELD

TABLE OF CONTENTS

(Please note that crayons or colored pencils are recommended.
The ink in markers will bleed through the pages)

YOUR NEW BOOK

I am honored, my heart swells with glee,

That you've chosen this book, a dream come to be.

I poured in my soul, a labor of love,

And I'm grateful to you for the push and the shove.

To thank you for choosing, a gift I'll bestow,

A $500 voucher, to help your dreams grow.

Freedom Publishing, a team of great might,

Will guide you along, and bring your dreams to light.

I've longed to publish, a dream oh so grand,

With Freedom and Amazon, my dreams in your hand.

Now I have liberty, to spend with my kins,

No more 9 to 5, my new journey begins.

The team at Freedom, professional and kind,

Their knowledge is vast, it opens the mind.

With them, everyday people can make a great start,

Build their own publishing empire, follow their heart.

I hope someday soon, your book I will find,

And help your dreams take flight, all intertwined.

Thank you again, for choosing this book,

I hope it brings you joy, at every look.

SCAN ME

INTRODUCTION

Welcome, dear reader, to this book of fun,

Full of puzzles and activities for everyone.

It's a memory book, you see,

For those with cognitive impairment, like me.

If you or a loved one has Dementia or Alzheimer's too,

This book is for you, to help your memory stay true.

You'll find crossword puzzles, word find, and connect the dot,

Plus other activities to help your memory not be forgot.

The rhyming directions will guide you through each ask,

Making it fun and engaging, an enjoyable task.

Whether coloring pages or a matching game,

Each activity can help your memory flame.

This book of puzzles is quite a delight,

Each one is solvable, not too tight.

Easy and 1,2,3, completing puzzles is a breeze,

With this new book, you're sure to please.

So let's dive in and see what this book has in store,

To help with cognitive impairment and so much more.

We hope you find joy, laughter, and fun,

In this Activity Memory Book for everyone.

ALPHABET TRACE

Hello, hello, my friend, today we'll trace each letter,

We'll study the image and begin to make each line better.

So let's get started, don't you worry about M, N or O,

With some patience and practice, soon you'll be a pro!

First, take a pencil or a crayon, whichever one you like,

And hold it nice and steady, then let it take flight.

Start at the top of the letter, and slowly trace down,

All the way to the bottom, and then around and around.

Great job, now you're tracing, you're doing really swell,

Remember to practice every day, and every night as well.

With time and patience, you'll see your letters become neat,

And your writing will be wonderful, just like a special treat.

So now you know how to trace, and you can do it with ease,

You're a smart and talented student, the best one with the keys.

Keep on practicing and you'll get better every day,

Who knows, one day you'll teach someone else this exceptional way.

Ant

Trace the uppercase and lowercase letters

A A A A A A A A A A

A

a a a a a a a a a a

a

Banana

Trace the uppercase and lowercase letters

B B B B B B B B B

B

b b b b b b b b b b

b

Cat

Trace the uppercase and lowercase letters

C C C C C C C C

C

c c c c c c c c c c c

c

Dd

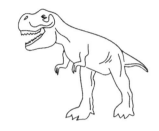

Dinosaur

Trace the uppercase and lowercase letters

D D D D D D D D

D

d d d d d d d d d

d

 **Ee**

Elephant

Trace the uppercase and lowercase letters

E E E E E E E E E

E

e e e e e e e e e e

e

Fish

Trace the uppercase and lowercase letters

F F F F F F F F F

F

f f f f f f f f f

f

Grapes

Trace the uppercase and lowercase letters

G G G G G G G G

G

g g g g g g g g g

g

Hen

Trace the uppercase and lowercase letters

H H H H H H H H H H H

H

h h h h h h h h h h

h

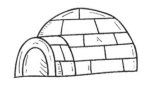

Igloo

Trace the uppercase and lowercase letters

I I I I I I I I I I I

I

i i i i i i i i i i i i

i

Juice

Trace the uppercase and lowercase letters

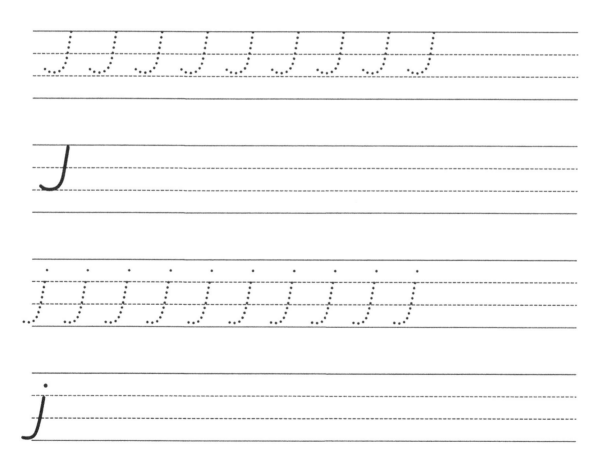

Kangaroo

Trace the uppercase and lowercase letters

K K K K K K K K

K

k k k k k k k k

k

Lion

Trace the uppercase and lowercase letters

 **Mm**

Mango

Trace the uppercase and lowercase letters

M M M M M M M

M

m m m m m m m m m

m

Nest

Trace the uppercase and lowercase letters

N N N N N N N N

N

n n n n n n n n n n

n

Orange

Trace the uppercase and lowercase letters

O O O O O O O O O O

O

o o o o o o o o o o

o

 **P p**

Peacock

Trace the uppercase and lowercase letters

P P P P P P P P P

P

P P P P P P P P P

p

Queen

Trace the uppercase and lowercase letters

Q Q Q Q Q Q Q Q Q Q

Q

q q q q q q q q q q q

q

Rose

Trace the uppercase and lowercase letters

R R R R R R R R

R

r r r r r r r r

r

 **Ss**

Swallow

Trace the uppercase and lowercase letters

SSSSSSSS

S

SSSSSSSS

s

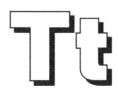

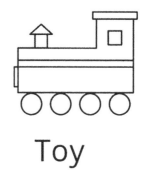

Toy

Trace the uppercase and lowercase letters

Umbrella

Trace the uppercase and lowercase letters

Van

Trace the uppercase and lowercase letters

V V V V V V V V

V

v v v v v v v v v

v

Watermelon

Trace the uppercase and lowercase letters

W W W W W W W

W

w w w w w w w w

w

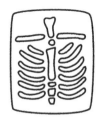

X-ray

Trace the uppercase and lowercase letters

X X X X X X X X X

X

x x x x x x x x x

x

Yoyo

Trace the uppercase and lowercase letters

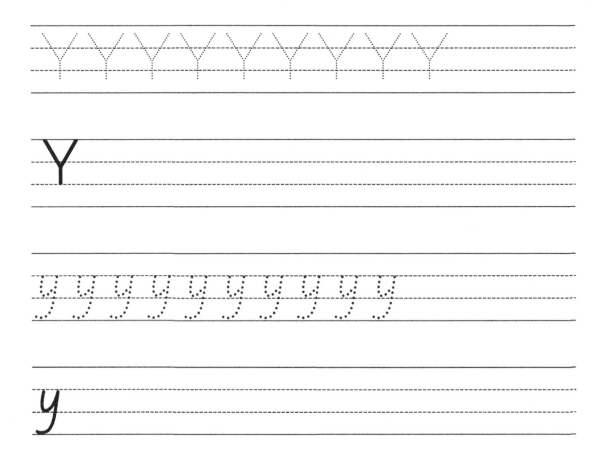

Zz

Zip

Trace the uppercase and lowercase letters

Z Z Z Z Z Z Z Z Z

Z

z z z z z z z z z

z

CONNECT THE DOTS

Start with a dot, then follow the line,

Connect each number, it's puzzle time!

From one to two and three to four,

Connect the dots, and you'll want more!

Soon you'll see a picture appear,

It's like magic as the dots draw near.

A masterpiece you will have found,

So much fun, you'll be astound.

Now that the dots are all connected,

It's time to admire the image reflected.

A picture has been revealed, oh so fine,

And it's all thanks to the number and line!

Dot-to-dot puzzles may be tall or small,

A challenge for one, or many or all.

So next time you're looking for something amid,

Try a dot-to-dot puzzle - you'll be glad you did!

Dot to Dot

Connect the dots to complete the picture

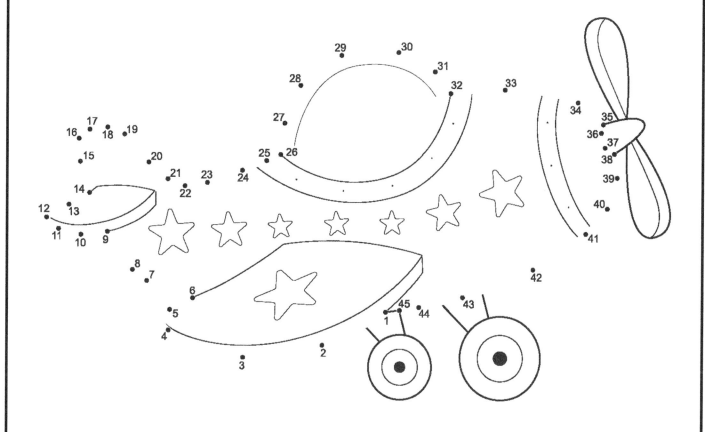

Dot to Dot

Connect the dots to complete the picture

Dot to Dot

Connect the dots to complete the picture

Dot to Dot

Connect the dots to complete the picture

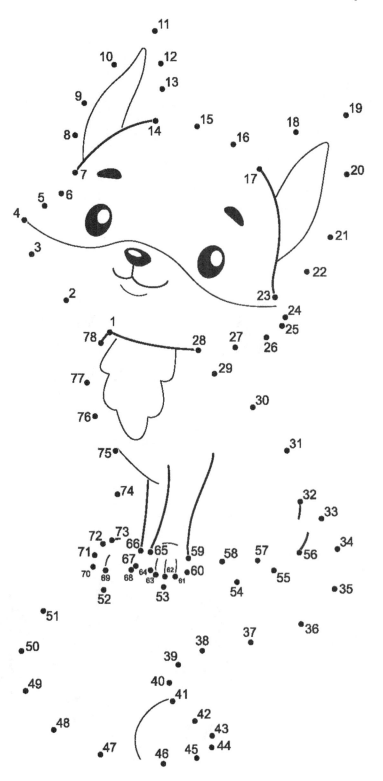

Dot to Dot

Connect the dots to complete the picture

Dot to Dot

Connect the dots to complete the picture

Dot to Dot

Connect the dots to complete the picture

Dot to Dot

Connect the dots to complete the picture

Dot to Dot

Connect the dots to complete the picture

Dot to Dot

Connect the dots to complete the picture

Dot to Dot

Connect the dots to complete the picture

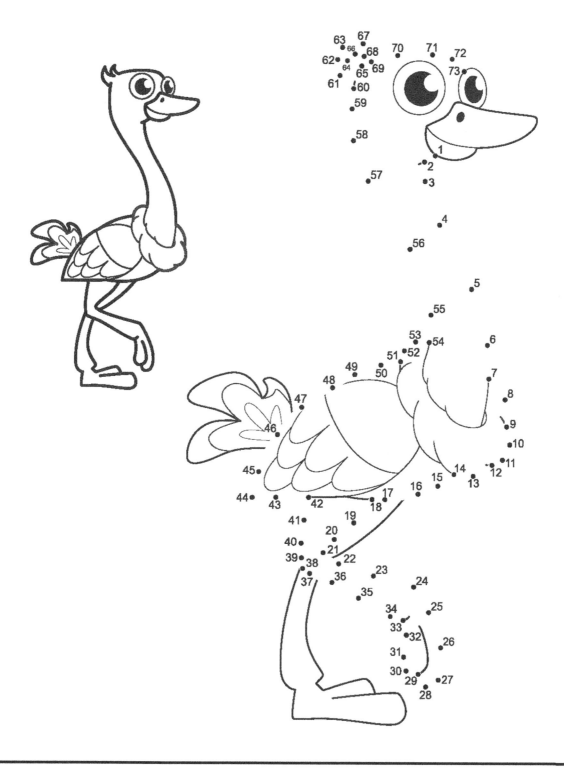

Dot to Dot

Connect the dots to complete the picture

Dot to Dot

Connect the dots to complete the picture

Dot to Dot

Connect the dots to complete the picture

Dot to Dot

Connect the dots to complete the picture

MAZE

It's a maze o'there, all twisty and turned,

Attempt it u'dare, and maybe get burned.

The goal is simple, it's plain to see,

Find your way out, and be set free.

Left or right, up or down,

Be sure to escape, with nary a frown.

Through corridors narrow, and passages wide,

You search for an exit, with nothing to hide.

Dead ends and traps, at most every turn,

Can make you feel like you've got more to learn.

But keep your cool, and stay on track,

Soon you'll find your way back.

Follow the clues, and use your wits,

You'll get out of there, as quick as a blitz.

Around the corners, and through the gates,

You'll emerge victorious, and one of the grates.

Some mazes may be tough, and sometimes mean,

But you can beat them, like a king or a queen.

So go ahead and give it your best,

You'll solve these mazes, and you'll pass the test!

Maze

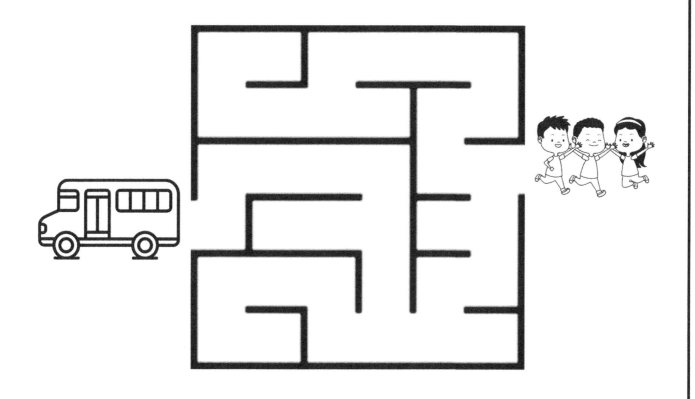

Maze

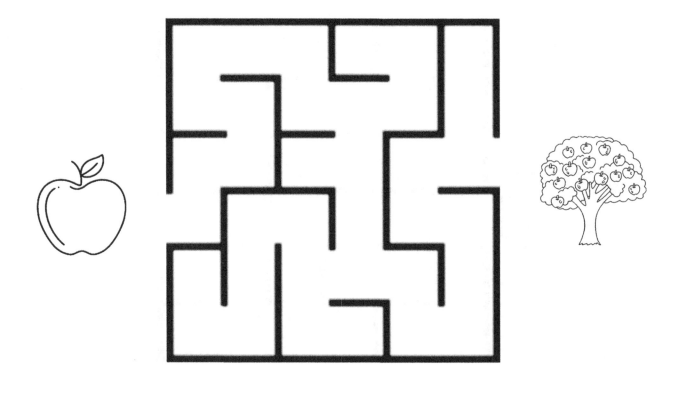

Maze

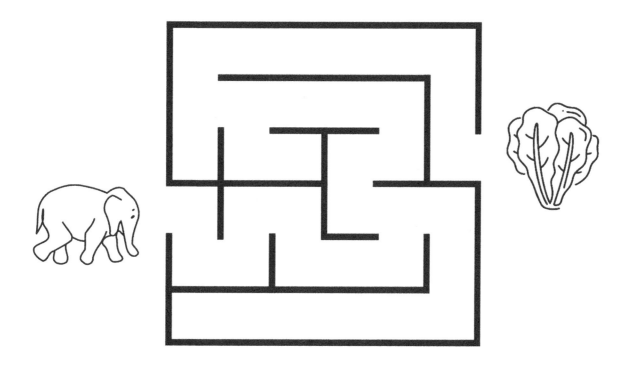

Maze

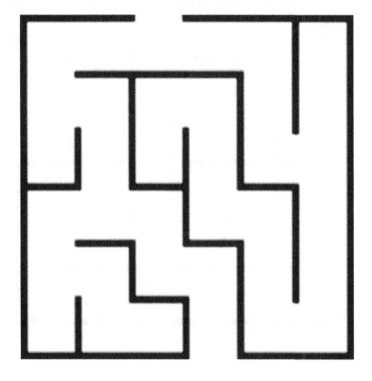

Maze

Maze

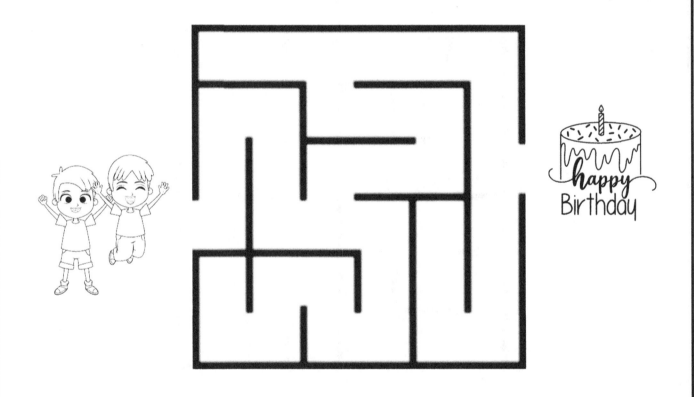

Maze

Maze

Maze

Maze

Maze

Maze

Maze

Maze

Maze

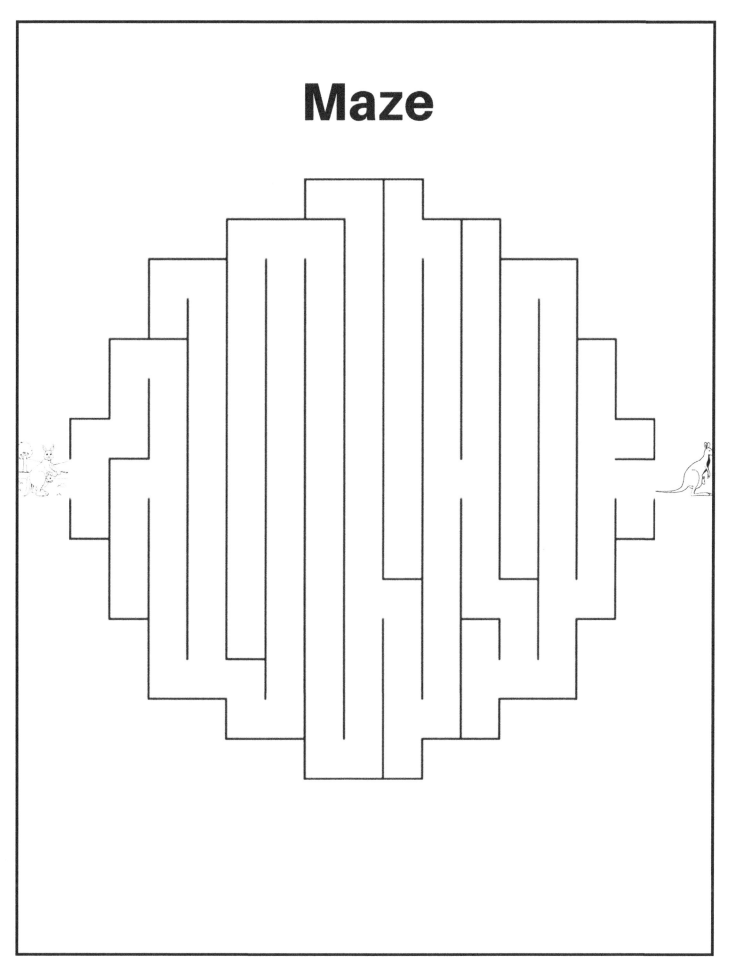

Maze

Maze

Maze

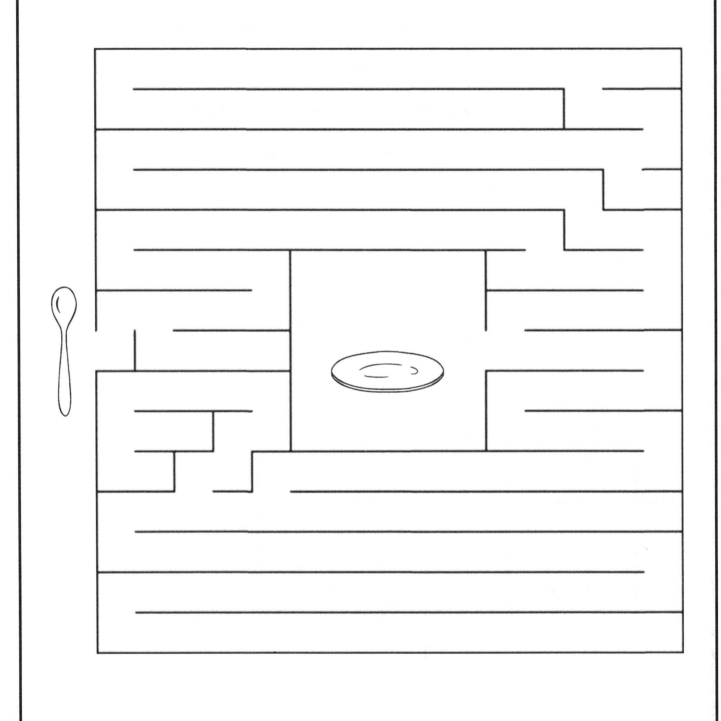

COLORING PAGES

Let me tell you folks, there's nothing like coloring with a crayon or pencil

It's a great way to relax, and it's oh so simple

But let me give you a tip, and I hope it's not too brash

Stay away from those markers, they'll make your coloring trash.

Now I know what you're thinking, "But markers are so bold and bright!"

Well, let me tell you, they're also messy and just not quite right.

They'll bleed through the page and ruin all the fun,

So stick to crayons or colored pencils, my friend, and don't be undone.

You can shade and blend with ease, and make your colors pop

Markers can't compare, they just fizz and then they flop

So if you want to color like a pro, and make your art stand out

Use crayons or pencils, and avoid those markers, without a doubt

In conclusion, coloring is a wonderful thing

It's a fun way to pass the time, and it can be quite calming

So grab crayons or colored pencils, and let creativity flow

And remember, when it comes to markers, just say no!

Alpaca

(Please note that crayons or colored pencils are recommended.
The ink in markers will bleed through the page)

Bear

(Please note that crayons or colored pencils are recommended.
The ink in markers will bleed through the page)

Cat

(Please note that crayons or colored pencils are recommended.
The ink in markers will bleed through the page)

Dog

(Please note that crayons or colored pencils are recommended.
The ink in markers will bleed through the page)

Elephant

(Please note that crayons or colored pencils are recommended.
The ink in markers will bleed through the page)

Fox

(Please note that crayons or colored pencils are recommended.
The ink in markers will bleed through the page)

Giraffe

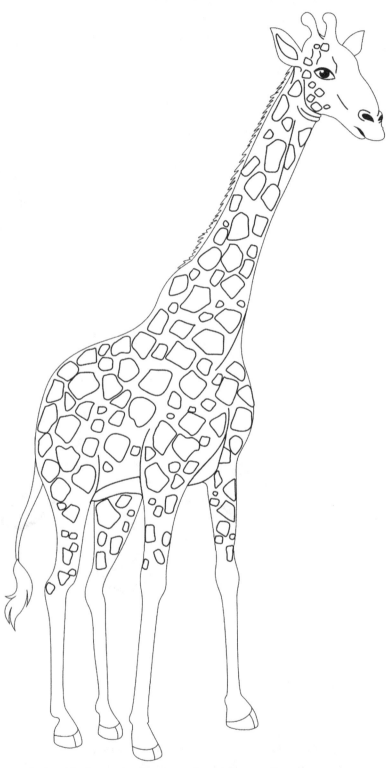

(Please note that crayons or colored pencils are recommended.
The ink in markers will bleed through the page)

Horse

(Please note that crayons or colored pencils are recommended.
The ink in markers will bleed through the page)

Iguana

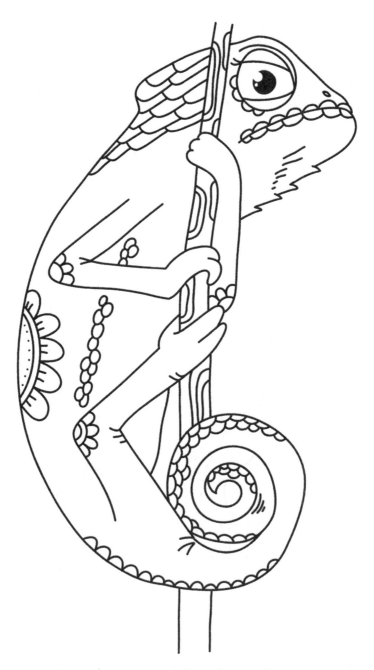

(Please note that crayons or colored pencils are recommended.
The ink in markers will bleed through the page)

Jellyfish

(Please note that crayons or colored pencils are recommended.
The ink in markers will bleed through the page)

Koala

(Please note that crayons or colored pencils are recommended.
The ink in markers will bleed through the page)

Loin

(Please note that crayons or colored pencils are recommended.
The ink in markers will bleed through the page)

Moose

(Please note that crayons or colored pencils are recommended.
The ink in markers will bleed through the page)

Narwhal

(Please note that crayons or colored pencils are recommended.
The ink in markers will bleed through the page)

Otter

(Please note that crayons or colored pencils are recommended.
The ink in markers will bleed through the page)

Penguin

(Please note that crayons or colored pencils are recommended.
The ink in markers will bleed through the page)

Quail

(Please note that crayons or colored pencils are recommended.
The ink in markers will bleed through the page)

Rabbit

(Please note that crayons or colored pencils are recommended.
The ink in markers will bleed through the page)

Squirrel

(Please note that crayons or colored pencils are recommended.
The ink in markers will bleed through the page)

Tiger

(Please note that crayons or colored pencils are recommended.
The ink in markers will bleed through the page)

Unicorn

(Please note that crayons or colored pencils are recommended.
The ink in markers will bleed through the page)

Vulture

(Please note that crayons or colored pencils are recommended.
The ink in markers will bleed through the page)

Whale

(Please note that crayons or colored pencils are recommended.
The ink in markers will bleed through the page)

Xerus

(Please note that crayons or colored pencils are recommended.
The ink in markers will bleed through the page)

Yak

(Please note that crayons or colored pencils are recommended.
The ink in markers will bleed through the page)

Zebra

(Please note that crayons or colored pencils are recommended.
The ink in markers will bleed through the page)

COUNTING ACTIVITY

Remember the Count,

Ready to teach you how to count an amount!

First, let's start with number one,

Counting is easy and lots of fun!

Two! Two numbers we can count,

We'll add them up, there's no need to doubt!

Three! Three numbers, what a delight,

Keep counting up and you'll get it right!

Four! Four numbers, don't be shy,

You're doing great, let's reach for the sky!

Five! Five numbers, oh what a feat,

Keep counting, soon you'll be complete!

Six! Six numbers, you're doing swell,

Counting is easy, can't you tell?

Seven! Seven numbers, let's keep going,

Counting up, your skills are showing!

Eight! Eight numbers, you're doing fine,

Counting up to ten, it's almost time!

Nine! Nine numbers, you're almost there,

Counting is fun, it's something we can share!

Ten! Ten numbers, we made it through,

Counting is something everyone can do!

So keep practicing and counting every single day,

And soon you'll be counting in every single way!

Addition

2	3	4	5	2
+2	+5	+4	+2	+3
4				

7	8	6	1	4
+3	+2	+2	+3	+2

4	8	6	2	5
+3	+1	+6	+5	+4

Addition

🧁🧁 + 🧁🧁🧁🧁🧁🧁🧁 = __

🧁🧁🧁🧁🧁 + 🧁🧁🧁🧁 = __

🧁🧁 + 🧁🧁🧁🧁 = __

🧁🧁🧁🧁 + 🧁 = __

🧁🧁🧁 + 🧁🧁🧁🧁 = __

🧁🧁🧁🧁🧁🧁 + 🧁🧁🧁 = __

🧁 + 🧁🧁🧁 = __

Addition

```
    5              □            11
  + □            + 1          + □
  ─────          ─────        ─────
    9              1            14


    □              □            □
  + 4            + 3          + 0
  ─────          ─────        ─────
    9              5            3
```

Addition

8 +2 ――― 10	7 +5 ―――	5 +4 ―――	3 +2 ―――	9 +8 ―――
7 +9 ―――	9 +2 ―――	4 +2 ―――	5 +3 ―――	4 +2 ―――
4 +7 ―――	8 +4 ―――	5 +6 ―――	7 +5 ―――	3 +2 ―――

Addition

🍎🍎 + 🍎🍎🍎 = __

🍎🍎🍎🍎 + 🍎🍎🍎 = __

🍎🍎 + 🍎🍎🍎🍎🍎 = __

🍎🍎🍎 + 🍎🍎🍎🍎 = __

🍎🍎 + 🍎🍎🍎🍎 = __

🍎🍎🍎🍎🍎 + 🍎🍎🍎 = __

🍎 + 🍎🍎🍎🍎🍎🍎🍎 = __

Addition

$$\begin{array}{r} 5 \\ + \boxed{} \\ \hline \boxed{10} \end{array}$$

$$\begin{array}{r} \boxed{} \\ + \boxed{1} \\ \hline \boxed{7} \end{array}$$

$$\begin{array}{r} \boxed{11} \\ + \boxed{} \\ \hline \boxed{12} \end{array}$$

$$\begin{array}{r} \boxed{} \\ + \boxed{4} \\ \hline \boxed{8} \end{array}$$

$$\begin{array}{r} \boxed{3} \\ + \boxed{} \\ \hline \boxed{4} \end{array}$$

$$\begin{array}{r} \boxed{} \\ + \boxed{0} \\ \hline \boxed{1} \end{array}$$

Addition

7	9	6	7	8
+7	+5	+5	+2	+4

8	9	8	1	7
+7	+2	+6	+9	+6

5	7	8	2	7
+9	+1	+8	+9	+9

Substraction

5	4	7	6	4
-2	-2	-4	-2	-3
1				

7	8	6	7	3
-5	-3	-5	-1	-2

8	8	6	5	8
-5	-8	-6	-1	-4

100

Substraction

Shade the number of fish to match the correct answer

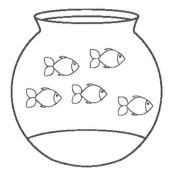

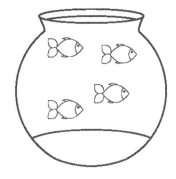

5 - 2 =

4 - 2 =

2 - 2 =

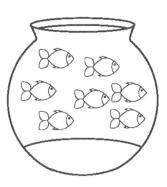

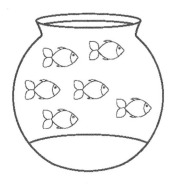

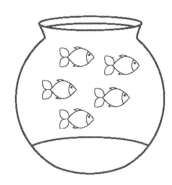

7 - 6 =

6 - 2 =

5 - 3 =

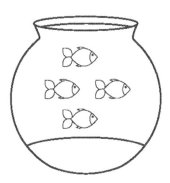

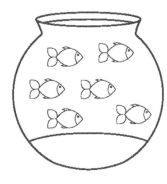

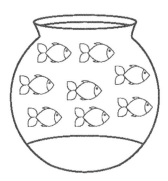

4 - 4 =

6 - 3 =

8 - 5 =

Substraction

 $5 - 2 =$

 $7 - 4 =$

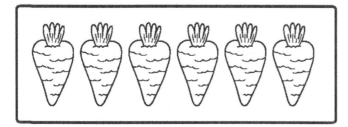 $6 - 1 =$

 $9 - 3 =$

 $3 - 3 =$

Substraction

Shade the number of circles to match the correct answer

5 - 2 = _____	⭕⭕⭕⭕⭕
3 - 2 = _____	⭕⭕⭕
4 - 1 = _____	⭕⭕⭕⭕
3 - 1 = _____	⭕⭕⭕
5 - 1 = _____	⭕⭕⭕⭕⭕
4 - 2 = _____	⭕⭕⭕⭕

Substraction

10 – 0 = ☐   5 – 4 = ☐

5 – 3 = ☐   2 – 0 = ☐

7 – 4 = ☐   4 – 1 = ☐

8 – 4 = ☐   1 – 0 = ☐

7 – 6 = ☐   5 – 1 = ☐

Substraction

3	3	4	5	5
-2	-2	-4	-2	-3
1				

7	8	6	3	4
-3	-2	-2	-1	-2

4	8	6	5	5
-3	-1	-6	-1	-4

Substraction

Shade the number of circles to match the correct answer

5 - 4 = _____	◯ ◯ ◯ ◯ ◯
3 - 1 = _____	◯ ◯ ◯
4 - 2 = _____	◯ ◯ ◯ ◯
3 - 2 = _____	◯ ◯ ◯
4 - 1 = _____	◯ ◯ ◯ ◯
3 - 2 = _____	◯ ◯ ◯

Substraction

7 − 2 = ___

5 − 4 = ___

3 − 3 = ___

4 − 1 = ___

6 − 1 = ___

6 − 3 = ___

5 − 3 = ___

CROSSWORD PUZZLE

In a crossword puzzle, there's so much to do,

Please fill in every space, by seeing each clue.

Horizontal, vertical, no objection too,

You must solve them all, and it's all up to you.

Write a word here, and another one there,

Fill in the boxes, and be sure to use care.

With every answer, difficulty is rare,

And soon you will finish, a wordsmith beware.

The pictures can be tricky, with some asking, why?

But you must persist, and not give a sigh.

With every guess and no alibi,

Complete the puzzle you will, none can deny.

Every letter counts, it's plain to see,

One little mistake, and you'll start over, gee.

But with every correct answer, you'll find a key,

To unlock this puzzle and set your mind free.

So go ahead, and give it a run,

With every clue, you'll feel that you've won.

And soon enough, you will be done,

A crossword puzzle champion, oh how much fun.

Cross Words

Cross Words

Cross Words

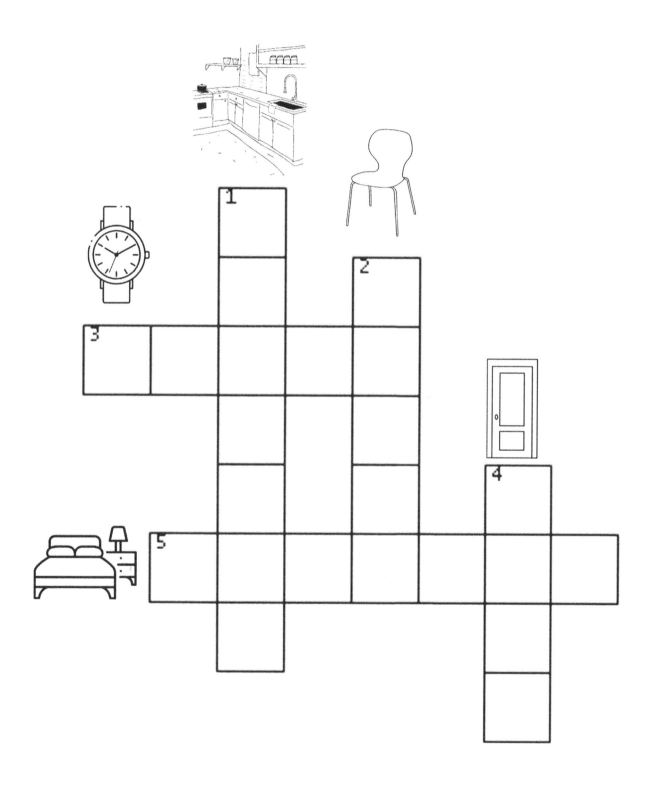

Cross Words

Cross Words

Cross Words

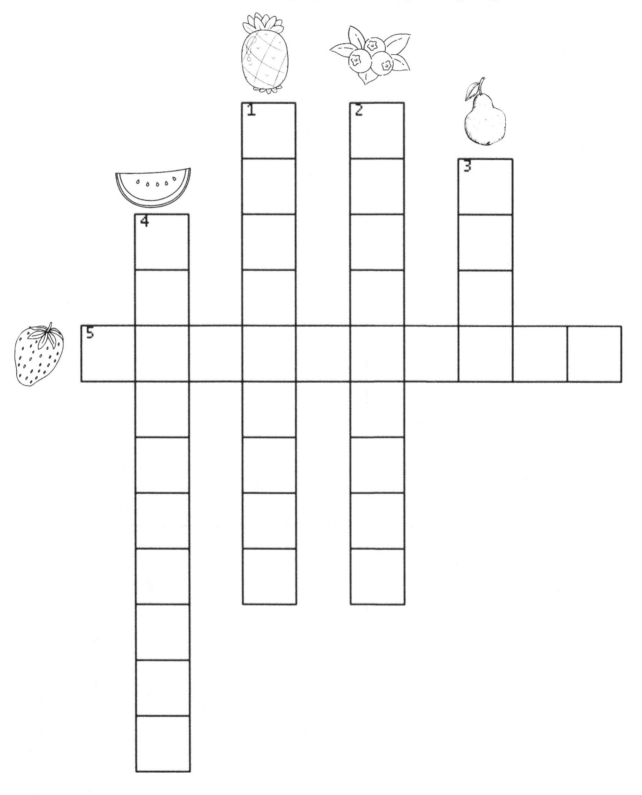

Cross Words

Cross Words

Cross Words

Cross Words

Cross Words

Cross Words

WORD SEARCH PUZZLE

A word search puzzle, let's take a look,

Words are hidden, like a secret book!

Your mission, should you choose to accept it,

Find all the words, and don't you forget it.

Across and down, diagonals found,

The words are hiding, hunt like a hound!

Keep seeking and searching, don't make a sound,

Soon enough you'll find them, they'll be circled and bound!

Word search

```
W F X H C I H Q X S S K C T H
L I F N C D Z D E B U P I Z I
R O N L M S G L P C R K N L V
Z Z F T O I B O C M H Q T M B
C L S R E A I R C E X L V Y U
L B A L T R V F L A P W Y K M
K D C E A T E M E X Y B L O Q
H W G S R M H Z M O T X B N V
S E R U S O I O P M C G R G F
V E T U T O C N P M E U Q W C
U T I E I F L C A I X B H T Y
Y I E H U C E G T A U R Z T O
T G Y F R R S R Y Z D L I B T
A O J P F S P P G D O G G D Z
R S U M M E R D P R A C F O D
```

ANIMALS	FRUITS	SUMMER
VEGETABLES	VEHICLES	WINTER

122

Word search

```
G  A  B  P  K  O  X  V  T  L  U  N  V  D  S
Z  K  R  H  Q  O  J  F  Q  Q  C  H  A  V  A
P  U  Z  F  N  G  O  X  R  Q  T  X  F  F  Y
S  C  H  O  O  L  H  B  A  J  V  M  J  U  R
O  L  S  B  R  Y  E  Y  E  C  W  T  A  P  W
R  A  F  U  V  N  I  E  K  B  E  M  J  R  I
W  R  S  M  P  F  S  G  W  Q  Y  P  Y  N  S
J  Y  E  I  L  T  G  B  C  X  Q  C  P  C  Z
I  W  N  W  R  V  T  S  N  P  L  E  I  Q  M
T  O  L  K  S  J  C  E  H  M  N  D  L  P  L
Z  I  M  V  J  P  X  U  A  R  W  G  O  E  Q
L  T  H  J  B  I  X  P  K  C  T  J  P  N  R
X  Y  F  M  U  H  V  M  F  D  H  G  I  C  D
C  G  G  L  S  Z  L  I  S  A  K  E  N  I  P
R  F  W  B  T  M  P  D  C  X  O  N  R  L  F
```

BAG	BOOK	PEN
PENCIL	SCHOOL	TEACHER

Word search

```
M O D A M M T K H A A D E B P
P W D O I O I Q U X B T E J V
A Z J P O T O N R F M N I K S
X X I V C R H R U D R P U N T
W B V H W F X B T G R C Z N J
T G E M L N V L F F H O S Q W
S N D H Q O F G H O M E R E I
P D H L H P S Z A M S E N
O T E R K D L D S Y R C V C D
V O A M E K F S X Q O U T O
M G H W X L P R A J V Q V X W
R O V X K B J U M Z P Z R G R
Q J M C L D Y G J U T Y L B N
N N Q F D D H E S N P X D X F
R R E U V S O X D A V I I G A
```

BED	DOOR	HOME
KITCHEN	ROOM	WINDOW

Word search

```
C O R E Y R J G D X N U L R W
Z A V Y U S H I A R K R U G U
J O R U Y X N Z C Q V N N G Y
L A J E S N U Y C Q V W C T T
K F S X E K Y A A P S Z H O L
B W V R B H Z U H N R G M D A
B G Q K G R F L E Q Y U W C H
K U M H A T W F X W R X H L H
N U S Y Z P T S T Q N V M A L
N O I V F V T O E D N U G V L
X T G X N R A B H Z E Y A F U
A T Z B D Y R K N R M U K D F
Z W E V J L U P Y R O O T H B
A H N Q S X R K M S M K D A X
F A M I L Y B B Y T N F D K M
```

CARE	DINNER	FAMILY
LOVE	LUNCH	MOM

Word search

```
J  R  B  Q  B  G  N  B  N  V  P  W  U  N  V
W  E  B  A  Y  X  A  F  O  H  A  Z  O  Z  U
A  F  G  O  N  N  Z  J  M  E  U  K  S  A  Q
X  F  E  N  A  M  E  C  E  S  U  P  X  H  P
A  D  T  N  A  D  E  K  L  R  A  E  G  S  F
U  G  A  H  B  R  Y  W  T  O  Y  H  P  H  J
S  J  T  B  O  N  O  W  M  W  N  M  L  Z  U
E  X  Y  J  V  C  D  I  C  H  W  G  X  S  Z
L  U  B  K  M  M  C  K  T  F  G  G  K  C  A
R  B  U  L  I  R  G  R  A  E  P  F  N  X  H
F  O  F  W  O  L  Y  A  K  R  A  N  T  E  O
C  P  O  G  Q  Q  S  D  I  S  P  U  Q  L  M
P  K  N  Z  U  Q  V  X  E  N  P  G  O  G  F
W  A  T  U  R  J  L  H  S  W  L  E  E  R  Q
M  Z  N  F  D  I  Z  Y  A  C  E  E  U  O  L
```

APPLE	BANANA	LEMON
MANGO	ORANGE	PEAR

Word search

```
Z  Q  M  B  F  G  G  H  P  R  P  Y  V  U  R
D  Z  T  P  N  V  S  D  B  W  L  L  N  F  F
W  T  V  K  J  A  F  R  H  N  D  T  H  Y  P
P  M  J  G  C  R  V  Z  I  O  B  F  J  P  K
W  I  H  F  O  V  G  F  A  L  I  F  U  W  H
J  I  N  W  X  G  Q  I  T  E  J  P  G  Q  J
H  F  B  E  X  U  X  Q  F  M  S  P  T  J  W
G  S  T  R  A  W  B  E  R  R  Y  O  H  V  B
Q  N  K  Q  R  P  X  F  P  E  O  Y  J  L  N
D  X  R  S  M  O  P  T  C  T  U  F  V  M  L
B  B  P  C  T  B  Y  L  Q  A  H  C  A  E  P
B  L  W  A  V  Q  Z  W  E  W  V  O  Y  Q  F
M  J  M  P  W  L  D  V  H  V  A  R  H  G  Y
V  O  X  U  O  S  T  Y  H  Y  F  A  S  I  G
T  A  D  V  L  U  R  A  E  Z  Z  Z  P  K  R
```

FIG	PEACH	PINEAPPLE
STRAWBERRY	TOMATO	WATERMELON

Word search

```
N Q C Y M O T A T O P F P W O
C O K U E R P A P P A F H W J
R U I Z Q C T U U T Q E L M F
Z K H N H I O D M N K O S Y A
N R Z M O H R I L P V C C E U
E S C T J V R Z M W K J P N W
P J P A Z O A S M F B I J Z W
A A M C G Q C G M Y B Z N K V
X L M O N L L E Q T D B W T O
G M I U Q F J D D Y T Q L O L
H K N T P M H V L D C L Z T R
V Q O M G Z R K A C V Q S P D
C U C U M B E R Y J A Y Q A Y
E O C R E R V E A C X E Z Z O
P Y B C F P H G Q P V F W D Y
```

CARROT	CUCUMBER	ONION
PEA	POTATO	PUMPKIN

Word search

```
H  R  I  C  U  N  C  U  L  J  Q  J  Y  T  C
X  J  O  O  W  P  Z  H  C  Y  S  R  B  O  P
H  R  Q  C  W  O  R  Y  I  E  R  I  D  F  M
A  E  Z  O  I  T  U  P  L  E  J  R  Y  S  F
F  Y  O  N  V  H  C  C  H  Y  C  K  F  U  J
H  T  U  U  S  Y  R  C  E  K  C  P  C  H  C
V  N  C  T  P  P  O  W  I  S  O  X  X  O  M
X  G  S  T  E  I  U  X  X  N  F  B  P  S  B
H  B  A  P  R  I  C  O  T  P  N  O  R  A  O
Y  V  K  E  A  G  N  M  W  G  L  B  U  K  Z
Y  V  R  J  R  N  O  L  E  M  F  U  M  W  N
E  Z  C  A  W  L  Z  W  I  C  P  F  M  W  T
C  U  P  G  M  Y  I  M  T  N  Q  E  Z  N  Z
O  E  Z  A  F  Z  L  M  S  M  P  S  V  Q  O
S  F  C  M  F  A  F  E  X  R  G  Z  U  L  P
```

APRICOT	CHERRY	COCONUT
GRAPES	MELON	PLUM

Word search

```
L C L R W B D S K F D P K X C
M A H P P M C Q V E R O J W I
G L J I B R Y Z Y A H K O M L
V A J N L B O Z D T H R L K R
Z F B H I I E I N X F A L X A
R W S K T R S H G C Q H K P G
H P N W Z H B R K G M G E Q R
Y C P S S P G E G D S K C E
C S H C R E G N I G I H K Q W
V K S X K B T D L T T Y H M F
N M S R U D V X M Z T C X T F
P V Z O N U R N Y K V L D S C
C G B J S N N P R T H C G L O
Z H C E U L U V A C L K I D X
U M B S U D S F F V D A F T I
```

| BRINJAL | CHILI | GARLIC |
| GINGER | OKRA | RADISH |

Word search

```
R  M  M  L  L  W  P  R  G  G  J  K  L  X  U
H  E  D  O  N  K  E  Y  M  M  W  W  T  D  E
U  O  G  V  N  G  K  L  P  L  U  G  W  R  Z
N  Y  G  I  D  K  B  J  F  S  V  Q  J  Z  P
A  I  L  Y  T  M  E  Z  A  Z  F  O  Q  A  B
V  L  L  X  F  I  J  Y  U  D  A  Y  B  Z  N
C  H  T  R  L  S  Q  N  X  A  A  G  W  V  P
K  A  F  R  U  U  M  I  E  A  N  U  V  S  B
C  B  E  E  A  R  N  N  P  Q  A  N  O  I  L
R  G  E  V  L  M  P  V  K  F  U  Z  U  V  Z
D  F  V  R  C  A  T  L  S  P  W  R  W  K  C
X  K  E  P  J  F  A  R  P  B  M  F  W  G  K
F  G  K  Y  H  C  P  N  Q  A  B  L  G  B  Z
J  O  R  Y  P  K  T  Z  C  U  A  Y  Z  D  U
J  D  X  Q  J  O  Q  V  W  Z  R  A  L  B  O
```

CAT	DOG	DONKEY
LION	MONKEY	TIGER

131

Word search

```
W  R  J  I  B  A  Q  B  U  Z  I  G  B  Z  A
Z  G  I  M  K  W  B  D  P  R  D  F  E  X  M
Y  X  Y  Z  L  X  B  C  J  T  V  Q  T  C  U
C  N  C  A  Q  T  S  Y  Q  J  N  T  A  O  N
V  R  W  L  C  Q  C  C  H  N  E  U  I  T  T
V  O  C  Y  D  A  B  N  X  S  B  U  N  A  J
T  B  K  N  T  Y  A  H  R  I  U  R  H  Z  P
V  W  R  E  G  F  F  O  U  M  F  B  V  P  E
T  G  U  T  L  P  H  C  V  I  F  S  F  Q  E
A  A  M  H  K  W  D  V  O  N  A  I  B  N  H
J  X  O  W  W  G  K  N  J  W  L  V  N  U  S
Z  V  G  G  Y  M  D  G  U  T  O  N  P  G  C
L  J  M  K  N  W  S  J  G  E  V  H  R  V  I
C  A  M  E  L  V  M  U  K  O  J  N  Z  K  Z
O  P  S  T  W  L  X  V  U  T  I  Q  V  I  S
```

BUFFALO	CAMEL	COW
GOAT	HORSE	SHEEP

Word search

```
T N A H P E L E T O F O D F R
G C W S C A J K D I A O X S Y
Z F W O W M T B Q L B Q X Q B
K P A H W U T B L X U B L X E
E C X Y S K H I A P O T A K Z
B D S W I O R B K A U W O R R
L F H G Z O S E P H N M M Q M
S Z H G G Z T G V J Y V F K E
T A S X G G D G B O H P E T W
C D D D U X Z K O D U O H S S
D N S C N H A V Y O D K B U C
S A B W H M E U G E Q S N H A
S P R A T B L M M V M J T C S
H A H Y A U V M N G Y V K I K
F E V S O E K P U I P V H F G
```

ELEPHANT	FOX	GORILLA
PANDA	RABBIT	RAT

133

TRACE THE LINES

Trace the lines, wise one,

Let your pencil lead you on the run.

Up, down, left, and right,

Stay within the lines, keep them tight.

A zig, a zag, a loop, and a twirl,

Draw a word and let it unfurl.

Stay within the lines, there's some work to do,

And soon you'll have a masterpiece, brand new.

An apple, an alligator, or an ant you'll see,

Draw something so beautiful as you are, we want to be.

Just follow the lines, and you'll see it through,

And create something beautiful, just like you.

Spelling Exercise

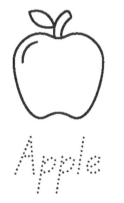
Apple

Alligator

Ant

Banana

Butterfly

Bear

Spelling Exercise

Cat

Car

Carrot

Dog

Doctor

Door

Spelling Exercise

Elephant   Eagle   Easter

Frog   Fish   Family

Spelling Exercise

Grapes

Guava

Ginger

Horse

Hen

House

Spelling Exercise

Igloo

Inkpot

Ice Cream

Jug

Juice

Judge

Spelling Exercise

Kk

Kangaroo

King

Kettle

Ll

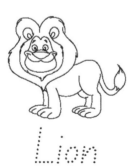
Lion

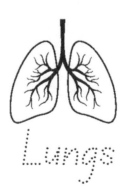
Lungs

Lemon

Spelling Exercise

Moon

Mango

Mouse

Nest

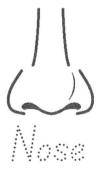
Nose

Net

Spelling Exercise

Orange

Ox

Onion

Panda

Peanut

Pigeon

Spelling Exercise

Queen

Quil

Quail

Rose

Rabbit

Rail

Spelling Exercise

Ss

Swallow

Sun

Sunflower

Tt

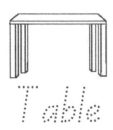
Table

Tomato

Teacher

Spelling Exercise

Unicorn

Umbrella

Uganda

Van

Village

Vegetables

Spelling Exercise

Ww

Watch

Wood

Window

Xx

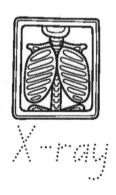
X-ray

Xylophone

Xyster

Spelling Exercise

Yoyo

Yak

Yogurt

Zebra

Zip

Zoo animal

WORD TRACE CURSIVE

To trace the words, start with fundamentals,

Circular shapes and curves are the instrumentals.

Place the tracing material flat on flat tables,

Hold the pen or pencil, as much as you're ables.

Guide your hand and trace the letters,

Build some confidence and trace them betters.

Don't worry if at first there's only onesies ,

Twenty-five more, and then you'll be donsies.

So keep practicing, and don't give up the funs,

With some persistence, you'll master it, one by ones.

Remember to offer praise and never fears,

You'll soon be tracing like seasoned pioneers.

With time and patience, your writing skill grows,

And then you'll be writing words like the pros.

Remember to be positive, kind, with cheers,

As writing words can be challenging for those in these years.

Aa Word Tracing Cursive

Trace the words in cursive for each picture.

Apple

Alligator

Airplane

Ant

Bb Word Tracing Cursive

Trace the words in cursive for each picture.

Butterfly

Boat

Balloon

Banana

Cc Word Tracing Cursive

Trace the words in cursive for each picture.

Cat

Carrot

Cake

Candy

Dd Word Tracing Cursive

Trace the words in cursive for each picture.

Duck

Drum

Dolphin

Donut

Ee Word Tracing Cursive

Trace the words in cursive for each picture.

Elephant

Eggplant

Earth

Eagle

Ff Word Tracing Cursive

Trace the words in cursive for each picture.

Flower

Frog

Fan

Fire

Gg Word Tracing Cursive

Trace the words in cursive for each picture.

Grapes

Giraffe

Guitar

Girl

Hh Word Tracing Cursive

Trace the words in cursive for each picture.

House

Hat

Heart

Hand

Ii Word Tracing Cursive

Trace the words in cursive for each picture.

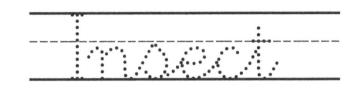
Insect

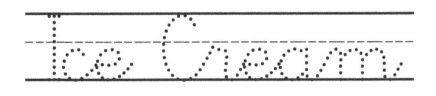
Ice Cream

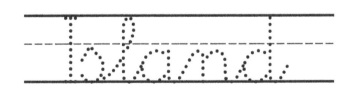
Island

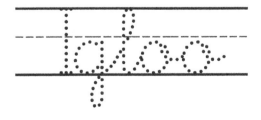
Igloo

Jj Word Tracing Cursive

Trace the words in cursive for each picture.

Juice

Jacket

Jellyfish

Jar

Kk Word Tracing Cursive

Trace the words in cursive for each picture.

Kangaroo

Key

Koala

Kiwi

Ll Word Tracing Cursive

Trace the words in cursive for each picture.

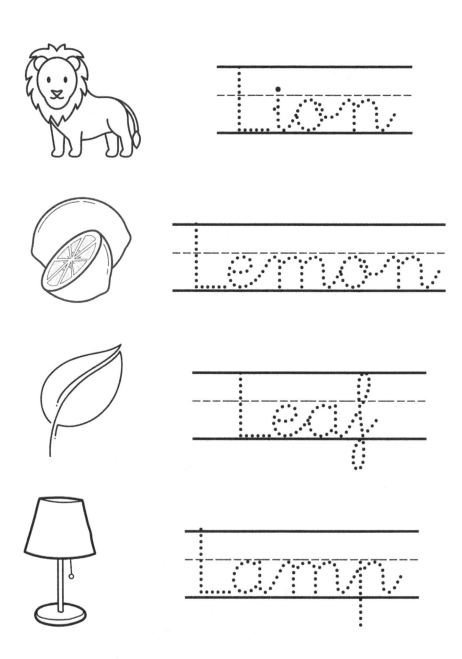

Lion

Lemon

Leaf

Lamp

Mm Word Tracing Cursive

Trace the words in cursive for each picture.

Moon

Monkey

Mug

Mouse

Nn Word Tracing Cursive

Trace the words in cursive for each picture.

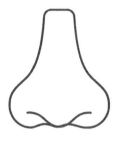
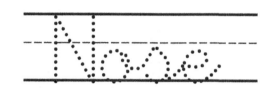
Nose

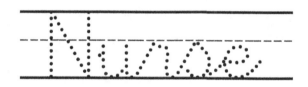
Nurse

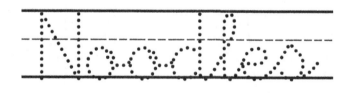
Noodles

Notebook

Oo Word Tracing Cursive

Trace the words in cursive for each picture.

Orange

Octopus

Oval

Owl

Pp Word Tracing Cursive

Trace the words in cursive for each picture.

Pan

Pineapple

Penguin

Pizza

Qq Word Tracing Cursive

Trace the words in cursive for each picture.

Question

Queen

Quail

Quiet

Rr Word Tracing Cursive

Trace the words in cursive for each picture.

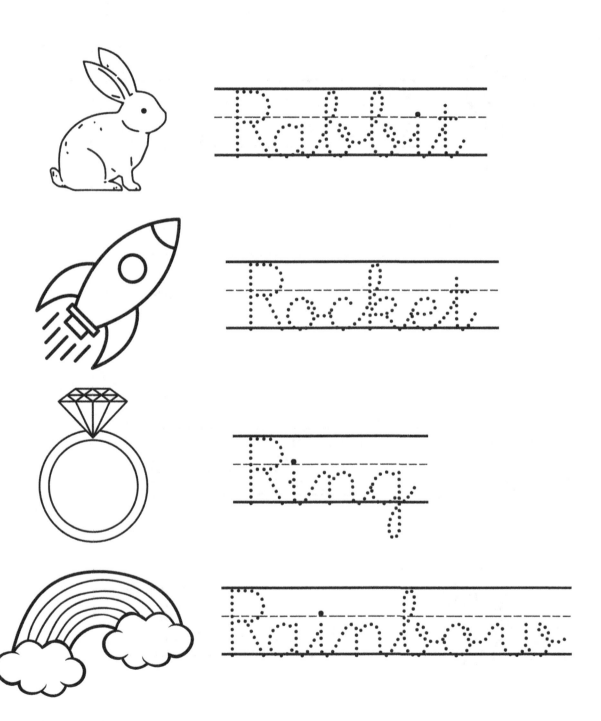

Rabbit

Rocket

Ring

Rainbow

Ss Word Tracing Cursive

Trace the words in cursive for each picture.

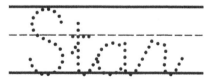

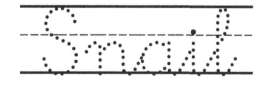

Tt Word Tracing Cursive

Trace the words in cursive for each picture.

Turtle

Truck

Tree

Table

Uu Word Tracing Cursive

Trace the words in cursive for each picture.

Umbrella

Unicycle

Uniform

Utensils

Vv Word Tracing Cursive

Trace the words in cursive for each picture.

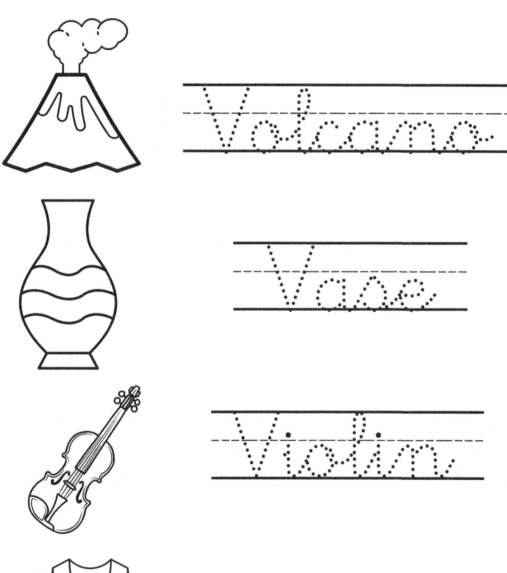

Volcano

Vase

Violin

Vest

Ww **Word Tracing Cursive**

Trace the words in cursive for each picture.

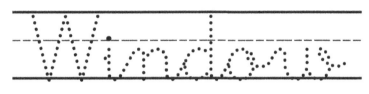

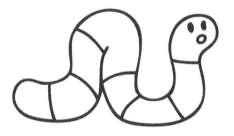
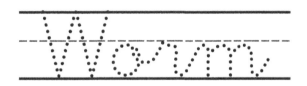

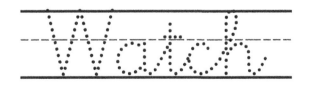

Xx Word Tracing Cursive

Trace the words in cursive for each picture.

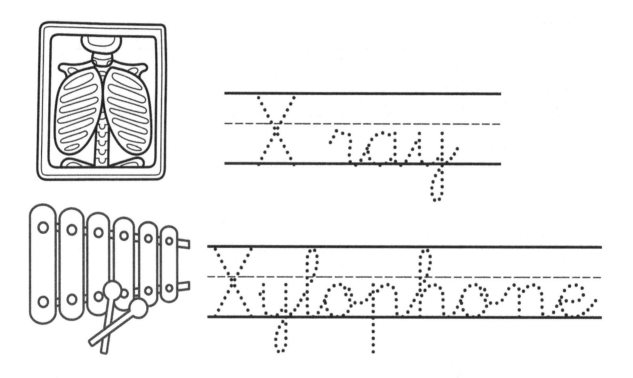

X ray

Xylophone

Yy Word Tracing Cursive

Trace the words in cursive for each picture.

Yak

Yacht

yo yo

Yurt

Zz Word Tracing Cursive

Trace the words in cursive for each picture.

Zero

Zebra

Zigzag

Zipper

MUSINGS AND MEMORIES

MEMORY AND WRITING ACTIVITY

Think back, think far, remember who you are!

A tale to tell, a story to share,

Of memories that you hold so fair.

Think of a day, a place, a friend,

Scribe a memory to comprehend.

With words and pictures, and rhymes so neat,

Tell us a story that can't be beat!

Who am I?_____

Remember a date_____/_____/_____

Remember a place_____

Remember a name_____

Tell the story_____

_____

_____

_____

_____

_____

_____

_____

_____

PHOTO AND WRITING ACTIVITY

An old picture, found in a book,

Possibly in a nook, come take a look!

A memory, a moment, captured in time,

A day that was special, oh so sublime.

Let's recreate that day, from so long ago,

Put on our thinking caps, and let the memories flow.

What did we wear? What did we do?

Let's bring it all back, for me and for you.

We'll find the props, and set-up the scene,

Recapture the magic, just like a dream.

We'll snap a new photo, to add to the pile,

And keep the memories with us, mile after mile.

For when we look back, at the times we all share,

We'll smile and remember the love and the care.

So let's recreate that moment, let's make it survive,

Keep that memory with us, forever alive.

Attached photo here

(Instructions: Using the photo as a guide, write down your memories or tell the story and have someone write the memory down for you.)

CHILDREN: A READING ACTIVITY

When we were young, we had so much fun,

Running around in the backyard under the sun.

We had no worries or troubles to bear,

All of our needs were met with loving care.

Our curious minds led us to explore,

Finding adventure and so much more.

Sometimes we stumbled, and got into strife,

But we always took responsibility for our life.

Our parents taught us to lend a helping hand,

To be kind and compassionate, always taking a stand.

They taught us to give without expecting a return,

A valuable lesson we continue to learn.

We made some friends who are dear to our heart,

Our bond is strong, when distance keeps us apart,

We long to visit them again someday,

To reminisce about memories at times fade away.

Oh, the memories we have of those precious years,

Filled with joy, laughter, and sometimes tears.

We'll always cherish them and keep them near,

As we journey through life and grow old in this sphere.

MIDDLE-AGE: A READING ACTIVITY

My dear child, how time has flown,

From infancy to now, oh how you've grown.

We worked hard, day and night,

To give you a life filled with love and light.

Life in the middle-age is a hustle and bustle,

Working hard to avoid any financial tussle.

We've raised you well, and taught you right,

Hoping that you'll be a beacon of light.

We've been to your school activities,

Cheered you on with heartfelt sensitivities.

Life can be so busy, we hope we did not miss,

Anything important, like your littlest bliss.

It's been a pleasure raising you to be so fine,

To watch you grow, and smile and shine.

Our love for you is beyond any measure,

And we hope we've given you the best life treasure.

GOLDEN YEARS: A READING ACTIVITY

Oh how time has passed, I've given it my all,

I've lived a full life, it's true, nothing small.

I'm old and frail now, but still have some zest,

To make it through each day, and do my best.

I'm so grateful for the love and care that you've shown,

Throughout all my life, the years better known.

The joy you've brought to my heart and soul,

Has made my life full, complete and now whole.

Now that I'm in my golden years,

I need a little help, and have no fears.

With love and grace, I'm asking for your aid,

To help me through the journey, now I'm afraid.

It's not easy to ask for help, I know,

But I trust you'll be there, with love, to show.

That no matter what, we're family, forever,

And we'll stand together, and never say never.

ME AND THEE:
A SPIRITUAL READING ACTIVITY

Tell a truth, thou art a soul of great worth,

Whose life doth pass like sand on the earth.

Thou knowest not the day nor the hour of thy passing,

But be assured, thy spirit shall endure, everlasting.

Thou must make good use of thy mortal time,

To fulfill thy purpose and reach for divine.

Seek ye first the kingdom of heaven,

And all else shall follow in the bread unleavened.

When thy final hour doth come to pass,

Fear not the journey that shall come to pass.

For thy spirit shall soar on wings like a dove,

And rest in the eternal embrace of a higher love.

Oh remember thou art a child divine,

And in eternity shall forever shine.

For in the presence of the Almighty thou shall surely be,

Thou shalt dwell in peace and harmony.

Fear not, for the trials of this earthly strife,

Shall be but a fleeting moment in the grand scheme of eternal life.

For when thou hast crossed the threshold of time,

Thou shalt enter a realm where love and joy eternally chime.

Thee, my dearest one, art thou so kind,

To spend this hour with me, in peace entwined.

Thou art a noble soul, a treasure rare,

Thou bringeth joy to me, beyond compare.

FINAL THOUGHT, ONE LAST RHYME

The time has come to end this rhyme,

But fear not, dear audience, I will once again chime.

I hope you had fun and enjoyed this time,

As much as I did, sharing my rhyme.

Thank you for listening, for being here,

For letting me speak and have no fear.

From the bottom of my heart, I say that it's true,

Thank you, oh thank you, to every one of you.

So let's end this rhyme on a very high note,

With a message of hope and love to promote.

May your days be filled with joy and cheer,

And until we rhyme again, farewell, my dear.

Answer Key

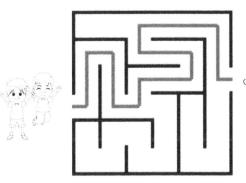

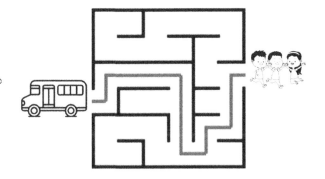

Answer key

Answer key

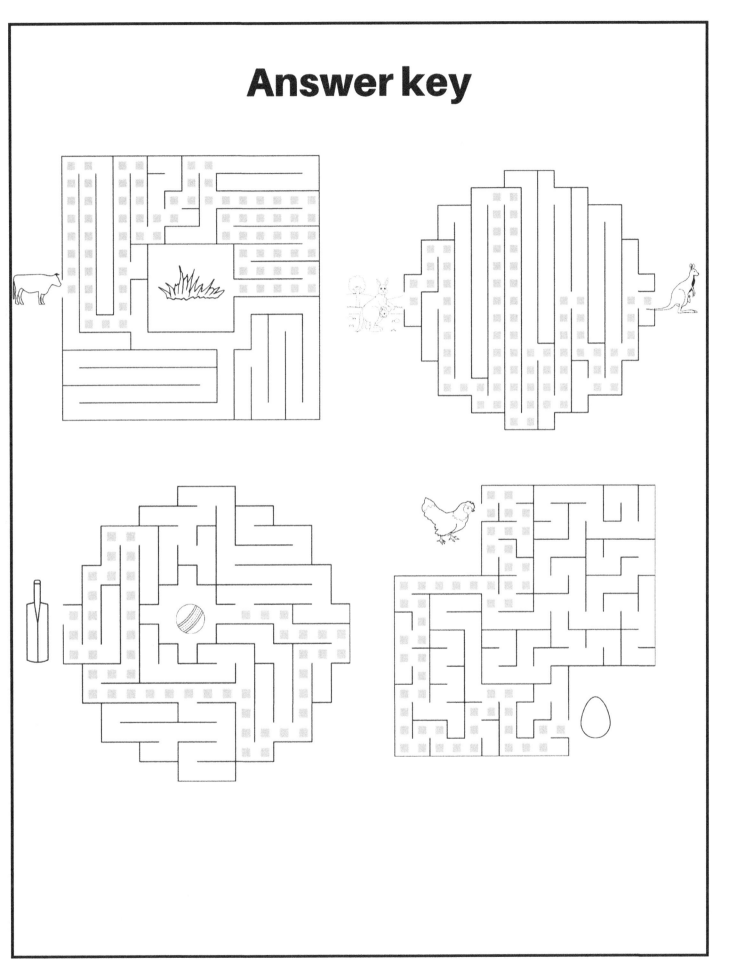

Answer key

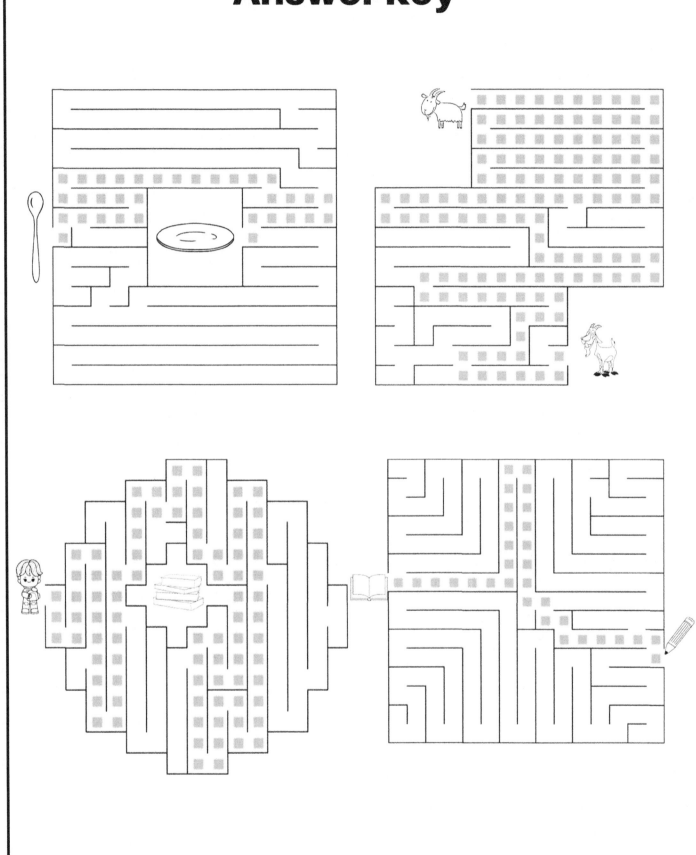

Cross Words answer key

Cross Words answer key

Cross Words answer key

Word search answer key

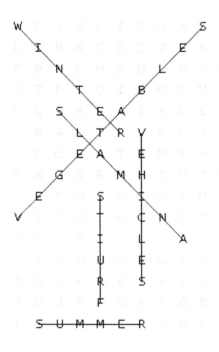

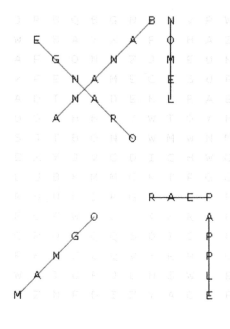

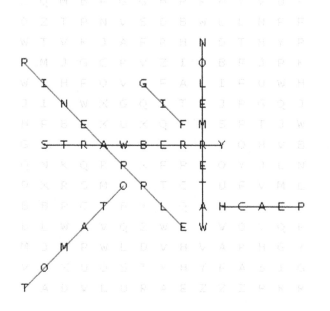

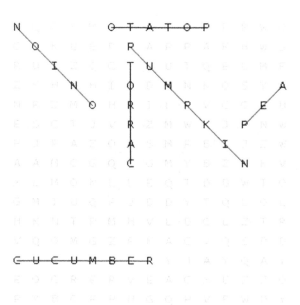

Word search answer key

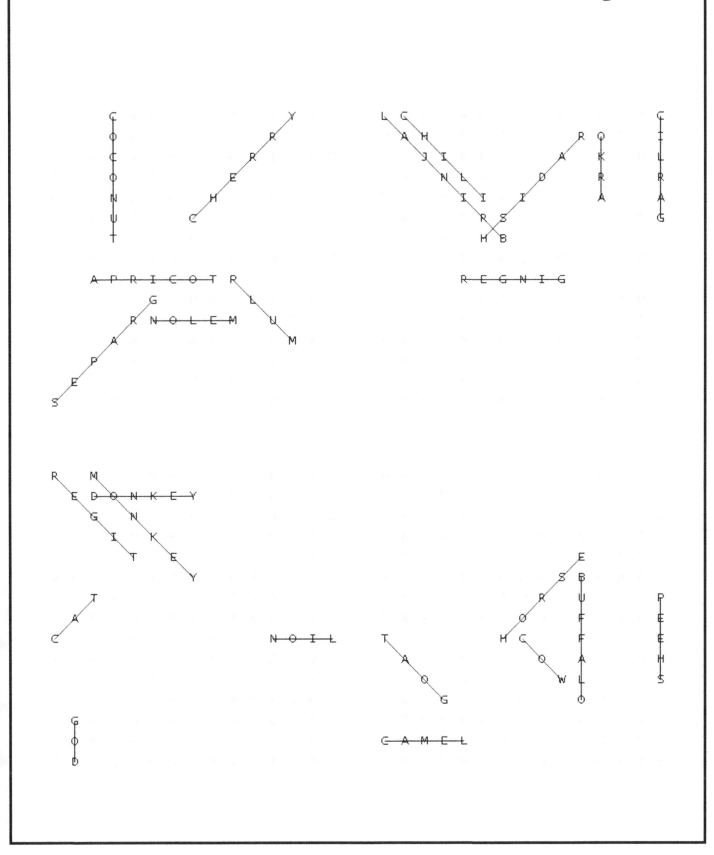

Word search answer key

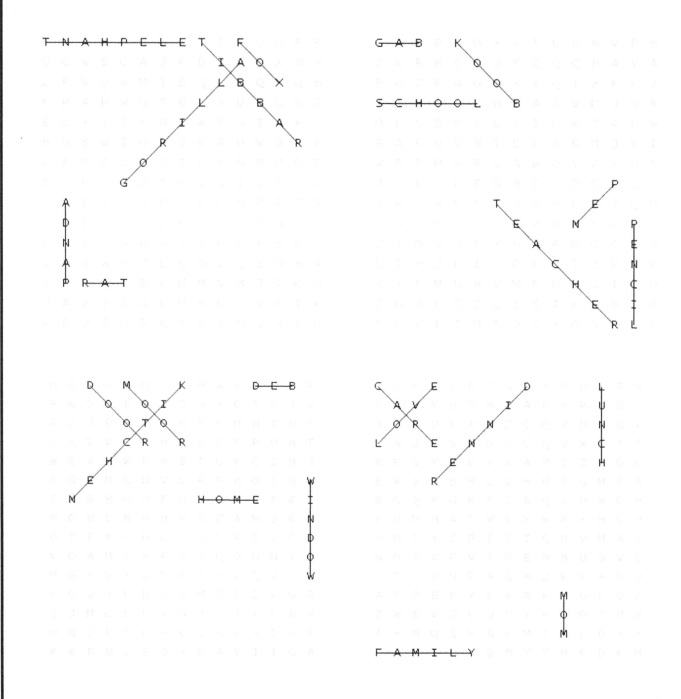

Made in United States
North Haven, CT
29 July 2023